PATH TO POWERFUL COMMUNICATION

*SIX STEPS FOR **EFFECTIVELY** PRESENTING YOUR IDEAS*

KIMALYSE POPKAVE, M.ED., CMI, CPPC
POSITIVE OUTCOMES PROFESSOR

Path to Powerful Communication

Six Steps for Effectively Presenting Your Ideas

KimAlyse Popkave, M.Ed., CMI, CPPC
Positive Outcomes Professor

ISBN: 978-1-7364464-2-3

kimalyse@keystoacademicsuccess.online
K. A. Popkave Consulting
Printed in the United States of America

ACKNOWLEDGEMENTS II

AUTHOR'S NOTE IV

INTRODUCTION 1

THE 3CS OF COMMUNICATION 8

THE BLUE STEP.................................... 14

THE WHITE STEP................................. 20

THE GREEN STEP 30

THE BLACK STEP 34

THE RED STEP 44

THE YELLOW STEP.............................. 54

REFERENCES 71

ABOUT THE AUTHOR 73

Acknowledgements

This book is dedicated to the memory of my mother, Liliana, who, through unconditional love and support, has always taught me to strive to be my best, and to my son, Chaim, who is my greatest inspiration and my raison d'être. Without their enduring love and understanding, this book would not have come to be.

This book is also dedicated to the students for whom it was originated as the *Path to Powerful Presentations*. Thank you for challenging me to explain concepts more visually.

Thank you, also, T. Falcon Napier. Your Native American wisdom has influenced me more than you know. I find myself referring to your teachings quite often, both when working with business clients and with academic students.

Author's Note

Very often, when faced with challenges, we need to ask for assistance to overcome these challenges and achieve our goals.

For assistance in becoming a more commanding communicator, please contact me. I am available for individual coaching, as well as for trainings and workshops.

To Your Success!!
Be *STELLAR*!
KimAlyse

KimAlyse Popkave, M.Ed., CMI, CPPC, LPDG
Positive Outcomes Professor
President
K.A. Popkave Consulting
570-617-6608
kimalyse@keystoacademicsuccess.online
www.keystoacademicsuccess.online

Introduction

One of my mentors, T. Falcon Napier, once said that Native American wisdom (he was Cherokee) teaches that when there are two concepts that each make perfect sense standing on their own, they can make even more sense when combined – the combined concept is stronger.

T. stated this, explaining that he combined the strategic thinking concepts in Dr. Edward DeBono's *Six Thinking Hats* (1985) with his own sales strategies and created a training tool for sales professionals that he called the *Path of Self Discovery*®. As an educator, the idea of combining concepts to strengthen student learning appeals greatly to me.

This book began as an explanation to my students during a public speaking class.

As I was explaining the process of developing a preparation outline for a speech, gleaned from Lucas (2001) and Logue, Freshley, Gruner, and Huseman, (1976) and many years of teaching speech courses at the college level, it became clear that some students were not understanding the concepts I presented. So, to clarify, I explained the process of the preparation outline as a path, following the color-coded thinking process first described by Dr. Edward DeBono in his book *Six Thinking Hats* (1985), and utilized in T. Falcon Napier's *Path of Self Discovery*®. By my color-coding the process of developing a preparation outline (gleaned from Lucas's *The Art of Public Speaking*), students had a more visual reference for the strategic thinking necessary to develop a speech. Of course, this same strategic thinking is not limited to speech preparation. It can be used for strengthening interpersonal communication and written communication, as well.

Many people have concerns about communication. Try as they might, they fall short of confidently achieving their communication goals. When reviewing their communication situations, they cannot figure out where they veered off course. What they do not realize is that when they are truly counting on accomplishing certain communication goals, if they fail to plan, they are truly planning to fail.

Yes, there is a six-step path to follow in creating powerful communication situations to convey ideas with *clarity*, *concision*, and *command*. This path journeys through six different modes of thinking, represented by six different colors: blue, white, green, black, red, and yellow. One should follow this path when using written and oral communication.

So, what modes of thinking do these colors represent?

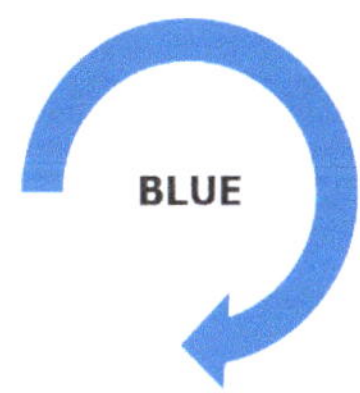

- The color of the sky on a beautiful autumn day – keeps thinking clear and crisp.
- Logical thinking to organize and focus the entire thinking process.
- Summarize information.
- Draw conclusions.

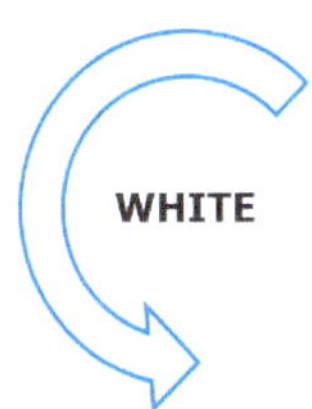

- The color of freshly fallen snow – what you see is what you see.

- Considers just the facts that are verifiable.
- Ask journalistic questions (who, what, where, when, why, how) here to gather all the facts.

- Originality and Imagination
- Feasibility is Not Required
- Options, Ideas and Alternatives
- Describes Desired Situation
- Identifies Goals

- The color of night and courage – a stimulus for change.
- Shows obstacles in one's path.

- Play "Devil's Advocate" here to gather more information.

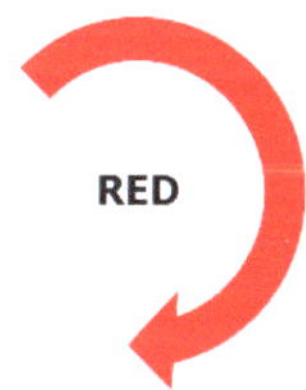

- The color of fire and passion.
- Deals with emotional connections to add persuasive strength.

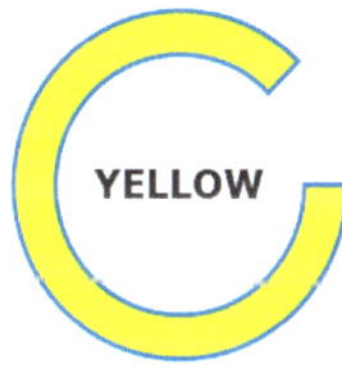

- The color of bright sunshine – sheds the light on the topic for the audience.
- Creates the desired situation.
- Application of these thinking strategies to communication preparation will yield conversations, presentations, and writing that are clear, concise, and

commanding, i.e. more productive to achieve desired results.

Before we explore this colorful Path to Powerful Communication, we must first consider the thread that runs through each step along this Path, the *3 Cs of Communication*: Clarity, Concision, and Command.

The 3Cs of Communication

During preparation and communication, stay focused by summarizing and drawing conclusions. In doing so, you will be able to convey your message using the 3 Cs of Communication.

Note: The following concepts have been adapted from Stephen E. Lucas (2001), *The Art of Public Speaking*, through several editions of the book.

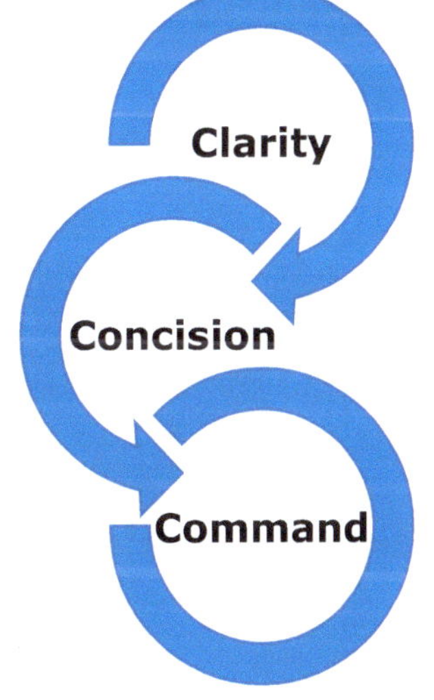

Clarity: State your message clearly.

Concision: State your case

simply. Avoid verbal clutter.

Command: State your ideas powerfully. When planning, take into consideration your audience. What is in it for them? Be certain to have all the facts. Also, consider the evidence: *examples*, *testimony*, and *statistics* are powerful clarifiers of communication. Lucas (2009) states that to be commanding, use sound reasoning, such as the following:

1. *Reasoning from specific instances*

   Reason from ***specific facts*** to a ***general conclusion***.
   Example:

   Fact 1: My physical education course last term was easy.
   Fact 2: My roommate's physical education course was easy.
   Fact 3: My brother's physical education course was easy.

Conclusion: Physical education courses are easy.

2. Reasoning from principle

Reason from a ***general principle*** to a ***specific conclusion***.

Example:

General Statement: All people are mortal.

Minor Premise: Socrates is a person.

Specific Conclusion: Therefore, Socrates is mortal.

3. Causal Reasoning

Seeks to establish a relationship between cause and effect.

Example:

There is a patch of ice on the sidewalk. You fall and break your arm. You reason as follows: "<u>Because</u> that patch of ice was there, I fell and broke my arm."

4. *Analogical Reasoning*

Reasoning in which a speaker compares two similar cases and infers that what is true for the first case is true for the second case.

Example:

If you are good at racquetball, you will be great at ping pong.

Note: It is most important to be certain the two items being compared are essentially alike. If they are, the analogy is valid. If they are not essentially alike, the analogy is invalid.

Watch out for logical fallacies. They will undermine your command. Logical fallacies are errors in reasoning. These errors should be avoided in speaking and writing. When listening to a speaker, keep alert for fallacies. Here is a basic list of logical fallacies to avoid:

- Hasty Generalization
- False Cause
- Invalid Analogy
- Red Herring
- Ad Hominem
- Either-Or
- Bandwagon
- Slippery Slope.

Note: To see how these fallacies are used, watch the videos, here: https://www.youtube.com/results?search_query=logical+fallacies+pbs

Now that we have considered the 3Cs of Communication, let's explore the colorful Path to Powerful Communication.

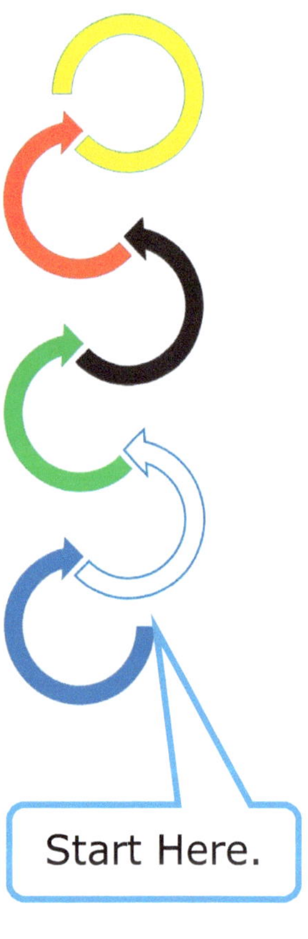

The Blue Step

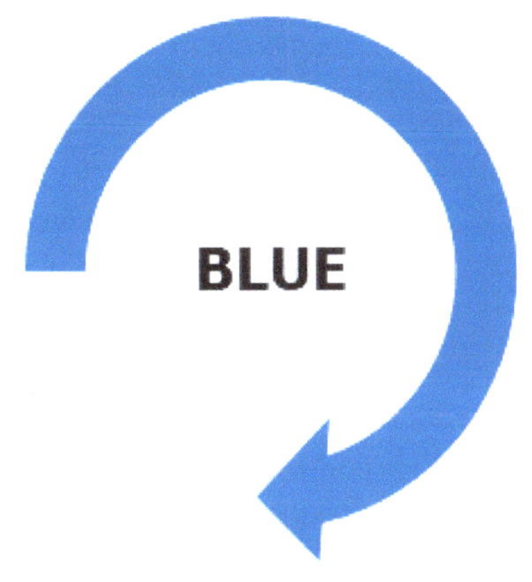

The first step along this path is the ***Blue Step***. Blue is the color of a clear sky on a crisp Autumn day. Blue Step thinking is clear and crisp. It is the logical phase that gets thinking *focused* and *organized* for clear communication. During Blue Step thinking, get organized by choosing the topic of the communication. Then, get focused by determining the general purpose. Is the purpose of the communication to inform, persuade, or entertain? All of this is done in planning for the communication. To achieve optimum results, plan for communication, whether oral or written, interpersonal or public.

> Remember, if you fail to plan, you are truly planning to fail.

Keep in mind this is about formal written and oral communication not spontaneous casual conversation. Let's look at a few examples of how this can be done.

Examples:

The examples below show Blue Step thinking in planning each of three types of communication: written, interpersonal, and public. In the Blue Step, consider the *topic*, the *general purpose*, and the *summary and conclusions* for each communication situation.

Written

- **Topic:** Assistance for Caregivers
- **General Purpose:** To inform
- **Summary and conclusions:** There are many home-based and community-based services available to assist caregivers in providing for loved-ones in their care. If one keeps the lines of communication open with other caregivers, one can find support groups that help ease the stress of caregiving.

Interpersonal (Conversation)

- **Topic:** Desideratum Tolerance
- **General Purpose:** To persuade
- **Summary and conclusions:** People should be more understanding, more respectful, and more appreciative of the similarities and differences of others. As Max Ehrmann (1927) said, "...With all its sham, drudgery, and broken dreams; it is still a beautiful world." Through Desideratum Tolerance, we can ensure life's beauty.

Public: (Presentation)

- **Topic:** Communication Strategies
- **General Purpose:** To inform
- **Summary and conclusions:** Following the strategic thinking process detailed in the *Path to Powerful Communication* will improve communication clarity, concision, and command when presenting.

So, here is your assignment:

Begin to plan a communication event (written, interpersonal, or public). Get <u>organized</u> by choosing a topic. If you do not have a topic in mind, Lucas (2001) suggests a brainstorming chart such as the one provided on the next page. List the first five ideas that come to mind for each category.

Then get <u>focused</u> by determining a general purpose (to inform, persuade, or entertain).

Topic Brainstorming Chart

Interests		Skills	
Experiences		Hobbies	
People		Places	
Events		Processes	
Plans and Policies		Natural Phenomena	

Please remember that Blue Step thinking can be revisited at any time to summarize and draw conclusions. Also, please remember to reflect on the 3Cs of Communication as you get organized and focused, and as you come back to the Blue Step to summarize and draw conclusions.

Now that we have organized and focused our thinking in the Blue Step, the next step along the *Path to Powerful Communication* is the White Step. We will explore this in the next chapter.

The White Step

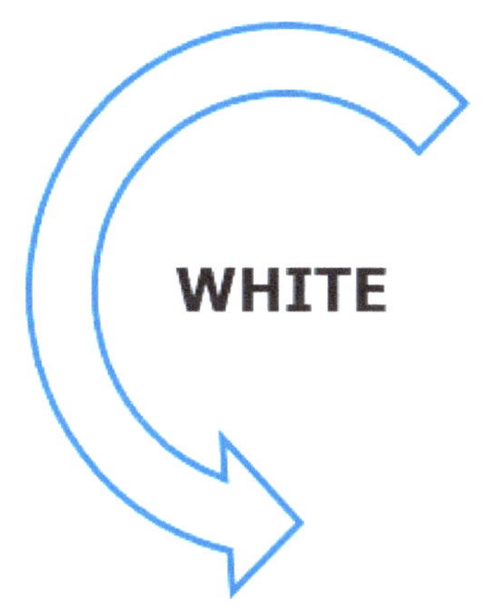

The second step along this path is the ***White Step.*** White is the color of freshly fallen snow. White Step thinking considers just the facts that are verifiable. In the White Step, we consider our audience. For whom are we writing? To whom are we presenting information? With whom will we be speaking? We must know our audience, if we are to communicate in a manner that will be clear and concise. Here we must consider the demographics of our audience. Consider the following analysis, as suggested by Lucas (2001):

Demographic Analysis

- Age: We think differently at different ages (A teenager will have different understandings of a topic than will someone in her 40's.)
- Gender: Men and women think differently on certain subjects. When speaking to a group of all one gender, the reactions a speaker gets from the audience may differ from the reactions that speaker would get when speaking to a mixed group. This is true for conversation as well as presentation. It is also true for written communication.
- Gender Preference: A person's gender preference can affect how a person receives and processes information.

- Racial, Ethnic, and Cultural Background: When communicating with a group of people that identifies with a specific race, ethnic group, or cultural group, do some research on what members of that group believe about your topic. When preparing to communicate with a group that is mixed racially, ethnically, and/or culturally, look for other similarities.
- Religion: When preparing to communicate with specific religious groups, realize that people allow their religion to shape their values, attitudes, and beliefs about certain topics.
- Group Membership: Group affiliation provides information about audience interests and attitudes surrounding certain topics.

Please realize that each of these demographics affects how your readers or listeners think. To gain insight into how the demographics affect audience thinking for certain topics, Google the demographic and the topic.

Example:

- Demographic: Jewish Religion
- Topic*:* Medical Ethics
- Google Results (a partial list):
  - Medical Ethics in Judaism | Jewish Virtual Library
    www.jewishvirtuallibrary.org/jsource/Judaism/medtoc.html
  - The Thirteen Principles of Jewish Medical Ethics
    www.science.co.il/Jewish-studies/Articles/Medical-ethics.php

- Judaism on Medical Ethics - A Collection of Questions and Answers
  www.chabad.org › Learning & Values › Questions & Answers

- Medical Ethics - Chabad.org
  www.chabad.org › Learning & Values › Ethics & Morality

Audience thinking is also shaped by the situation in which the communication occurs. Consider these elements of the communication situation. Here, Lucas (2001) suggests:

Situational Analysis

- The Size of the Audience: One individual with whom you are conversing, or an audience of 1,000 individuals

- Physical Setting of the Communication: Consider Time (early morning, afternoon, late evening), Location: indoors, outdoors, hot and humid, cold
- Audience Disposition toward the *Topic*: How much knowledge of the topic do they have prior to the communication?
- Audience Disposition toward the *Speaker*: What do they already know of and feel for the speaker?
- Audience Disposition toward the *Occasion*: Is it a special occasion? How do they feel about the communication situation?

In considering these elements of the communication situation, we will better understand the audience's thinking, to ensure clear communication.

After carefully considering the audience, it is equally important to consider the topic. Remember, in White Step Thinking, we are focused on just the <u>facts</u>. Gather facts and figures. What facts do you already have? Is further research necessary? Be certain to consider and use only information that is unbiased; make no judgments and form no opinions at this point. Consider the Present Situation from the perspective of readers and listeners. What does the audience already know of the situation? What do they need to know? In considering all of this, you will be better prepared for clear communication.

So, here is your White Step assignment:

Go back to the topic you chose in the Blue Step. Is your intent to inform, persuade, or entertain? Will this communication be written, interpersonal, or public? Who is your audience for this communication? Do a demographic Analysis and a Situational Analysis to get all the facts about your audience. The charts on this page and the next will help you organize this.

Demographic Audience Analysis	
Age	
Gender	
Gender Preference	
Racial, Ethnic, Cultural Background	
Religion	
Group Membership	

Situational Audience Analysis	
Size of Audience	
Physical Setting	
Audience Disposition towards Topic	
Audience Disposition towards the Speaker	
Audience Disposition towards the Occasion	

Now that you have analyzed the audience for your communication, do you have all the facts about your topic? If so, *GREAT*! If not, you may need to do some research. As you list the facts that you already know, and as you do further research on your topic, remember the 3Cs of

Communication. Strive for facts to add <u>clarity</u> to your communication. Express these facts <u>concisely</u>, and the communication will be <u>commanding</u>. So, start by listing facts about your topic that you already know. List them in the space provided.

Topic	
Fact 1:	
Fact 2:	
Fact 3:	
Fact 4:	
Fact 5:	

Now that we considered "Just the Facts, Ma'am, just the facts" in the White Step, let's continue along the Path to Powerful Communication with the Green Step.

The Green Step

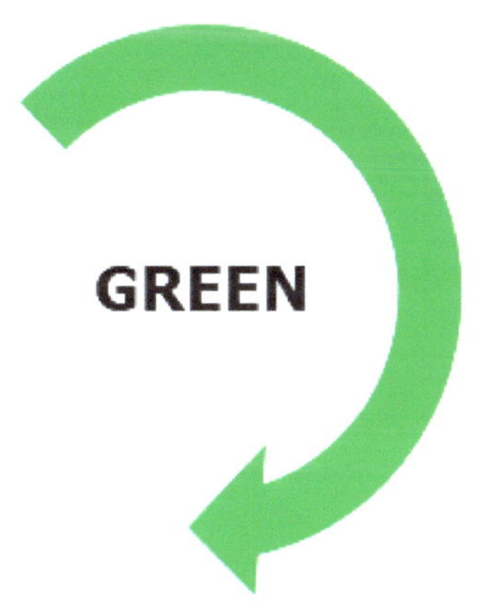

The third step along this path is the ***Green Step***. Green is the color of grass, plants, and things that grow. Green Step thinking deals with the fertility of the creative mind. In the Green Step, consider the *goals* of this communication. What ought to be achieved in this communication situation? What should the audience know, believe, feel, or do, after experiencing the writing, oral presentation, or conversation?

Touching back on the Blue Step for a moment, what is the General Purpose? Consider the audience and focus on the narrowed topic. Putting these three elements together, you will have the Specific Purpose. For example, in writing this book, my Specific Purpose is:

> *To inform my audience (academic students and businesspeople wanting to communicate more powerfully) of a six-step path to powerful communication*.

Now that we have considered communication goals, describe the Desired Situation. Define this clearly. Exactly what must occur because of the communication? Visualize the desired outcome Explore any options, ideas, and alternatives. Through clear visualization, the desired situation can be successfully created.

Having a clearly focused specific purpose will allow communication to be clear and concise. Clear visualization of the desired situation will help you achieve communication goals. Just remember the 3Cs discussed earlier: Clarity, Concision, and Command.

So, here's your assignment:

State a clearly focused Specific Purpose (goal) for the communication you began planning in previous steps. Then, clearly visualize and describe the desired situation – the desired outcome.

Specific Purpose:	

Visualization: Desired situation

Now that you have clearly defined the specific purpose and the desired outcome of the communication, consider feasibility by continuing along the Path to Powerful Communication with the Black Step.

The Black Step

The fourth step along this path is the ***Black Step***. Black is the color of night and the color of courage. In the Black Step, we do a rational negative appraisal. We consider what's wrong with this situation. But it is not a bad thing. It is just for the sake of information. Here we consider the feasibility of the desired situation, considering the present situation.

In Black Step thinking, we play devil's advocate. What obstacles can prevent achieving the desired situation? Here we need to consider the risks, dangers, and faults. However, we do not argue in the Black Step. At this point, consideration of risks, dangers, and faults is purely informational.

The strategies in Black Step thinking allow one to conduct a feasibility study for the communication situation. When considering the desired situation, do so from the standpoint of the Present Situation. How feasible is the desired situation, given the present situation?

Example:

> Joseph, a realtor for Century 21, has been with the company for five years. Over the past two years, sales from his office have dropped by 25%, from previous years. Century 21's national conference will occur in two months' time. During the conference, Joseph will

be meeting with company corporate executives to suggest a plan to get his office back on track. Using Black Step thinking strategies, he considers the following:

Present Situation	Real estate sales have dropped by 25% over two years' time. There is a staff of five real estate agents working from the office. Three agents are experiencing a low sales closing rate on properties they are showing.
Desired Situation	Within one calendar year, increase sales by 35%, up 10% from these past two years. All five agents will increase their sales closing rates by 10% or more.

Next, Joseph considers the feasibility of his desired situation, given the present situation. He takes a cold, hard look at this, and asks whether it seems feasible that his office will achieve the desired situation, given the present situation. Then, Joseph borrows a strategy from Toyota and does a "five-why analysis", asking "*why*?" about the answer. He asks the question "*why?*" five times – answering each "*why?*" about the answer to the previous "*why?*". In this way, Joseph drills down to the root of the problem (Liker, 2004). In comparing the present and desired situations, he determines what seems to be missing from the present situation.

Next, to get a clear picture of the obstacles to successfully increasing sales, Joseph lists the risks, dangers, and faults that have created the present situation and stand in the way of achieving his desired outcome.

Note: Please see the chart on this page and the next.

Goal:	Within one calendar year, increase sales by 35%, up 10% from these past two years; all five agents will increase their sales closing rates by 10% or more.
	Obstacles
Risks:	Less experienced agents have decreased sales closing rates. How can Century 21 corporate help alleviate this?
Dangers:	It is not currently a "buyer's market". Mortgage rates have

	increased slightly. People are not willing to view home ownership as an investment. Instead, in this economy, they view it as an expense. In other communities, it is a buyer's market.
Faults:	Economy is down. With the current political environment, the economy could continue to decline. The housing market could drop further.

Joseph wonders how he can successfully communicate all of this to the Century 21 Corporate Executives and gain their assistance to fully develop a plan to accomplish his sales goals.

After performing this rational negative appraisal and considering all the negatives that are preventing accomplishment of communication goals, it is time to reconsider the Specific Purpose for the communication. Revisions may be necessary. This is a big step in preparation for communication that is clear, concise, and commanding.

So, here's your assignment:

For your planned communication situation, use Black Step strategies to do a Rational Negative Appraisal. Begin by considering your present and desired situations, consider the feasibility of the desired situation given the present situation, then look at the Specific Purpose of your communication. From there, consider the risks, dangers, and faults that are the obstacles in the way of achieving your communication goal. Then, revise your specific purpose, accordingly. Space is provided here for your Black Step strategies.

Present Situation	
Desired situation	

Specific Purpose	

	Obstacles
Risks	
Dangers	
Faults	

Specific Purpose: (revised)	

Black Step thinking has revealed the obstacles to achieving the desired situation, and you have reconsidered your Specific Purpose. Now, it is time to explore emotional connections for persuasive power in the Red Step.

The Red Step

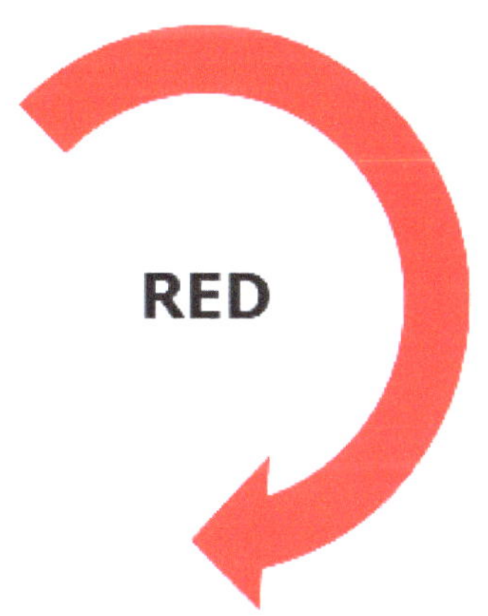

The fifth step along this path is the ***Red Step***. Red is the color of fire and passion. Red Step thinking deals with emotional connections to add persuasive strength to communication. In the Red Step, we consider the stakes for the audience if we don't accomplish the specific purpose. Questions to consider here are:

- What is the audience's emotional attachment to the present situation?

- Will the audience remain stuck in the present situation? Is this a bad thing?

- How will the audience feel if they remain in the present situation?

In the Red Step, one must also consider one's own emotional connection to the topic and Specific Purpose. Examine the following:

- Personal Experiences
- Feelings and Emotions
- Hunches and Intuition
- Opinions and Interpretations

Explore these in depth to evaluate for persuasive strength. Doing so will increase not only the persuasive strength of ideas, but also their clarity and concision.

For example, in writing this book, my target audience consists of academic students and businesspeople who must communicate powerfully interpersonally, publicly, and / or in writing. As I have previously stated, my specific purpose is:

> *To inform my audience (academic students and businesspeople wanting to communicate more powerfully) of a six-step path to powerful communication.*

So, what is at stake, if this book misses its mark and does not accomplish this purpose? On the next page, let's consider this from the reader's perspective, first.

Audience Attachment to the Specific Purpose	
What are the readers' emotional attachments to the present situation?	Readers are searching for ways to increase the success of their communication. For example, a college student needs to write a research paper that is clear, concise, and very persuasive. His grade in the course depends upon this research project. Another example is the financial services professional desperately seeking improvement in her sales closing rate. These readers have a clear emotional connection to their present situations.
Will the readers remain stuck in the	If the readers mentioned above do not find solutions to their present communication

present situation?	issues, they may remain stuck in the present situation.
Is this a bad thing?	For them, yes this is a bad thing. The college student must improve his written communication to present a research project that will earn him a top-level grade in the course and move him forward to graduation. The financial services professional is in danger of losing her career if she does not improve her closing rate.
How will readers feel if they remain in the present situation?	The college student will feel as if he is failing, if his communication remains as it is. The financial services professional is terribly upset and worried that, perhaps, she has chosen the wrong career path.

Now, let's consider emotional attachments from the perspective of the communicator – in this case, from this author's perspective.

My Attachment to the Specific Purpose	
Personal Experiences	A great part of my professional experience has been in the field of communication. I have taught communication courses (interpersonal, public, and written) at the college level for more than thirty years. I have worked with business executives, teaching the art of presentation.
Feelings and Emotions?	I feel very strongly that people must improve their communication skills, if they wish to create success for themselves, whether at

	the academic level or in their professional careers. It is also my strong feeling that many relationships of a personal and of a professional nature would be markedly improved if people would make a concerted effort to communicate more consciously.
Hunches and Intuition	Even though many people are fearful of communicating publicly, whether from the standpoint of doing presentations or from the standpoint of writing for an audience, my intuition tells me that secretly they crave being able to provide value to others through communication.
Opinions and Interpretations	Thinking strategically to plan for communication will allow anyone to communicate with clarity,

	concision, and command. The six modes of thinking, represented by the color steps, will allow anyone to successfully plan communication and get ideas across more powerfully.

So, here's your assignment:

Apply the power of Red Step thinking to your planned communication situation. Be as thorough as possible, to plan for persuasive strength (command). Explore both the audience's attachment to your Specific Purpose and your attachment to it. For your convenience, space is provided on the following pages for you to do this.

Audience Attachment to the Specific Purpose	
What are the readers' emotional attachments to the present situation?	
Will the readers remain stuck in the present situation?	
Is this a bad thing?	
How will readers feel if they remain in the present situation?	

My Attachment to the Specific Purpose	
Personal Experiences	
Feelings and Emotions?	
Hunches and Intuition	
Opinions and Interpretations	

Once Red Step thinking is complete, it is time to "shed light" on the topic for your audience. We do this in Yellow Step thinking.

The Yellow Step

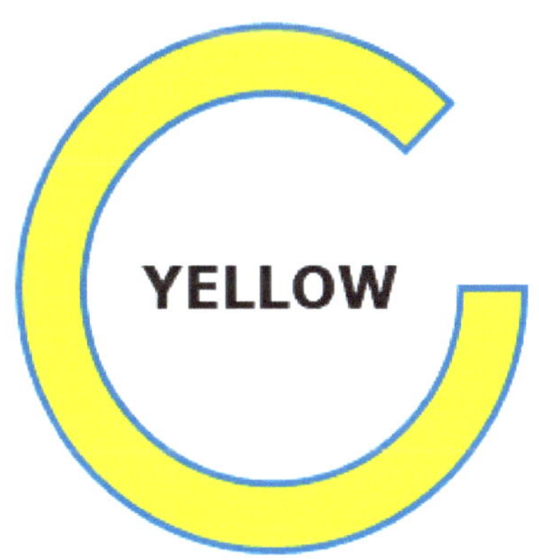

The sixth and final step along this path is the ***Yellow Step***. Yellow is the color of bright sunshine. The Yellow Step "sheds light" on the topic for your listeners and readers.

In the Yellow Step, we do a rational positive appraisal. We look at what's right with this picture. Here we explore processes, solutions, benefits, and values to formulate our main and supporting points.

Main Points:

To formulate main points, realize that they are the central feature of your communication. Therefore, select them carefully to accomplish your goals. Understand that clear structure is crucial to the understandability of your points. Part of this is limiting the number of main points to two or three. Another element of clear structure is the organization of your points. Lucas (2001) reminds us to organize main points strategically, in accordance with the purpose of the communication. So, what is this strategic order of main points? Lucas (2001) suggests the following:

- Chronological Order: Use this to tell when something occurred.
- Spatial Order: Use this to tell where something is.
- Causal Order: Use this to tell what caused an event to occur.

- Problem-Solution Order: Use this to tell about the existence of the problem and to suggest a solution.
- Topical Order: Use this to divide the main topic into subtopics.

For example, whether conversing, presenting, or writing, if the topic is voting, main points may be arranged as in the following examples:

- Chronological Order
  I. The 15th Amendment to the U. S. Constitution granted all U.S. citizens the right to vote regardless of race, color, or previous condition of servitude.
  II. The 19th Amendment gave women the right to vote.

III. The 24th Amendment ended the practice of poll taxing, forcing people to pay a tax to vote. (Coopman and Lull, 2012)

- <u>Spatial Order</u>
  I. The election's title and description are at the top of the ballot.
  II. How to complete the ballot is explained next.
  III. Candidates, proposals, propositions, and initiatives are listed in a specified order.
  IV. Space to record your vote is usually to the right of each item. (Coopman and Lull, 2012)
- <u>Causal Order</u>
  I. Local and state governments oversee voting procedures.
  II. Variation in voting standards has led to ballot counting problems at the national, state, and local levels. (Coopman and Lull, 2012)

- Problem-Solution Order
    I. Many people don't vote because they have difficulty getting to their polling places on election day.
    II. Alternative voting methods, such as mailed ballots, will solve the problem of not being able to get to the polls. (Coopman and Lull, 2012)
- Topical Order
    I. Philippines has 24 members of the Senate and 292 members of the House of Representatives.
    II. South Africa has 400 members of the National Assembly
    III. Australia has 76 members of the Senate and 150 members of the House of Representatives.
    IV. United States has 100 members of the Senate and 435 members of the House of Representatives. ("Table of voting systems by country", 2016)

Central Idea

During this process of formulation of points, the Central Idea, or thesis of the communication, becomes clear. This is very important in written communication as well as in public communication. In conversation, it is generally not regarded as imperative; however, if the conversation will be of a particularly important nature, it is a good idea to plan for a Central Idea.

Example:

You are planning a conversation with your employer, to negotiate for a raise in salary. While just asking for more money may not convince your employer that a raise in salary is warranted, focusing on what you have done to earn that raise may prove more convincing. For example, your central idea for this communication situation could be:

> During the past six months, I have developed a sales strategy that has increased company-wide sales by sixty percent, and I have landed three new national accounts; therefore, I am asking for a twenty percent raise in my annual salary.

Of course, in a situation such as this, it will also be helpful to show your employer the documentation of your sales strategy and the results, as well as the national accounts.

So, here’s an assignment:

For your planned communication situation (interpersonal, public, or written), consider two or three main points that will accomplish your specific purpose. Consider, also, how they will support a central idea or thesis for your communication. State your central idea and list your main points in the space provided.

Central Idea	
Main Point #1	
Main Point #2	
Main Point #3	

Supporting Points

Remember that without support, main points cease to be main points and are merely unsupported assertions. Unsupported assertions seriously deplete the clarity, concision, and command of your communication. Supporting details are the "*so what*" of communication. To paraphrase Lucas (2009), good communication is not comprised of generalizations or oversimplifications. The disadvantage with writing generalizations is that others in the communication situation are left wondering, "*So what?*".

To increase the clarity, concision, and command of your communication, choose supporting materials that are *accurate*, *relevant*, and *reliable*. Use examples, statistics, and testimony to support your main points. In doing so, you will increase the informative or persuasive strength of your main points, and more successfully accomplish your communication goals. (Lucas, 2009)

Note: For more information on using these supporting materials, please watch the video:

Supporting Materials

https://www.youtube.com/watch?v=PDn6J3RaVwE

Now, it is time to consider the supporting materials for your main points. What examples, statistics, and/or testimony will you use? Space is provided here for your convenience:

Support for Main Point #1	
Support for Main Point #2	
Support for Main Point #3	

Introduction and Conclusion

Now that you have planned your main and supporting points, to truly succeed, you need to create an *intriguing introduction* and a *compelling conclusion*. While you may be aware that you need to do this in preparation for written communication and for public speaking, you may not be as aware that you should do this when planning a conversation, as well. How you introduce and conclude your message may very well affect the success of your conversation. Therefore, you need to pay attention to creating your introduction and conclusion to have the greatest impact on those in your communication situation.

Creating the Intriguing Introduction

Let's delve into creating intriguing introductions. Why create an intriguing introduction? What will this do for your communication?

An *Intriguing Introduction* does the following:

- Creates a favorable impression and boosts your self-confidence
- Gains audience attention and interest
- Reveals your topic
- Avoids confusion
- Establishes your credibility and good will
- Previews body of presentation
- Gives audience something for which to listen

Just remember to be brief and creative when devising your introduction. Also, remember that for ease of design, create your introduction after your main and supporting points have been prepared.

Example:

So how can you plan an introduction for a topic of conversation? Let's re-visit the example of renegotiating salary.

> Hello, Mrs. Harcourt. Thank you for agreeing to speak with me. As I mentioned on the phone, I believe it is time to discuss my contributions to Harcourt International. Five years ago, I joined the Harcourt Team, and, as you know. I have taken on increasing responsibility. I know that we are close to the contract re-negotiation period, and that is why I want to speak with you.

Now that you have created an *intriguing introduction* to powerfully impact your audience's attention, it is time to turn your attention to creating a *compelling conclusion*.

Creating the Compelling Conclusion

To be compelling, the conclusion should end the presentation on a strong note. The conclusion signals the end of the communication and reinforces listener or reader understanding of and commitment to the central idea. A call to action can be included here, if one is appropriate.

Remember to be brief in concluding. Nothing weakens audience commitment to the central idea faster than a conclusion that seems to go on ad-nauseam!

Be creative in devising the conclusion. End with a ***bang***, not a whimper. Create a conclusion that will capture the minds and hearts of the readers and listeners and leave a lasting impression. Make the communication memorable.

So, here's an assignment:

Once again considering your planned communication situation, carefully create an intriguing introduction and compelling conclusion. Keep in mind the length of your communication (interpersonal, public, or written). The intriguing introduction should be no more than ten to twenty percent of the total communication time. The compelling conclusion should be no more than five to ten percent of the communication.

Intriguing Introduction	

Compelling Conclusion	

Polishing Your Communication:

Editing and *Revising*

When communicating in writing, it is time to edit and revise the writing, to be certain that it follows the 3Cs of Communication and that it is free of errors in spelling, grammar, and punctuation that can mar the clarity of the communication. Be certain that all the information being presented is correct. Revise, accordingly, and submit a clean copy — the finished product. Remember, your Integrity is showing.

In taking this time to prepare for your communication, you are following the path to powerful communication. The result is that you are communicating with clarity, concision, and command. You are successfully achieving your communication goals.

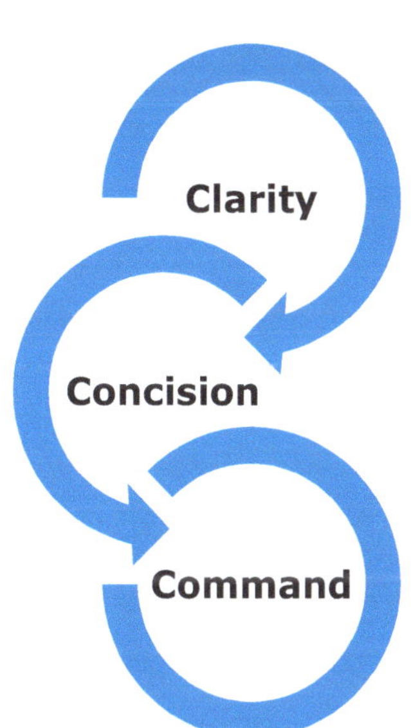

References

Coopman, S. J., & Lull, J. (2012). *Public speaking: The evolving art* (2nd ed.). Boston, MA, USA. Wadsworth Cengage Learning.

DeBono, E. (1985). *Six Thinking Hats*. Boston. Little, Brown.

Liker, J. K. (2004). *The Toyota Way: 14 Management Principles from the World's Greatest Manufacturer*. New York. McGraw-Hill.

Logue, C. M., Freshley, D. L., Gruner, C. R., and Huseman, R. C. (1976). *Speaking: Back to Fundamentals*. Boston. Allyn and Bacon.

Lucas, Stephen E. *The Art of Public Speaking*. Boston. McGraw-Hill. 2001. Seventh Edition.

Lucas, Stephen E. *The Art of Public Speaking*. Boston. McGraw-Hill. 2009. Tenth Edition.

Popkave, K.A. (2021). *Four Keys to Success: Leadership Strategies for Life's Projects*. Pottsville, Pennsylvania. K A Popkave Consulting.

Popkave, K.A. (2020). *Keys to Academic Success: A Guide to Achieve Stellar Performance*. Pottsville, Pennsylvania: K A Popkave Consulting.

Supporting Materials. (2013, August 20). Retrieved from https://www.youtube.com/watch?v=PDn6J3RaVwE

Table of voting systems by country. (2016, August 19). Retrieved from https://en.wikipedia.org/wiki/Table_of_voting_systems_by_country

About the Author

KimAlyse Popkave,

M.Ed., CMI, CPPC

Positive Outcomes Professor

KimAlyse Popkave is an educator. That is not just what she does, that is how she defines herself. With a Master of Education Degree in Speech Communication and Theatre Arts, KimAlyse is an accomplished leader with more than 30 years' experience as a professor, developing and implementing courses customized to reach specific objectives. Her specialties include strategic communication, strategic leadership, and student success. She has taught in a variety of academic settings, from elementary level to university courses at Penn State University and various Community Colleges, as well as in corrections education for both the Federal Correction system and the Pennsylvania Department of Corrections.

As an educator, KimAlyse has nearly 30 years' experience in business, as well. Earning her designation as a Certified MasterStream® Instructor, from the Tension Management Institute in 2002, enabled KimAlyse to develop programs for and work with businesses to help increase their bottom line and achieve their positive outcomes.

As a coach, consultant, trainer, author, and speaker, KimAlyse is dedicated to a clear mission: to help others to be successful. In addition to serving in these roles, KimAlyse has held the positions of Director of Learning and Communication for B.O.U.N.C.E. of Central Pennsylvania and Strategic Learning Technologist for the Shinshuri Foundation.

www.ingramcontent.com/pod-product-compliance
Lightning Source LLC
LaVergne TN
LVHW052256100826
845147LV00001B/63

9781736446423